ROMANS

HE READS TRUTH

HOW TO USE THIS BOOK

Each book in the He Reads Truth Legacy Series™ provides space to read and study Scripture, make notes, and record prayers. As you build your library, you will have a record of your Bible-reading journey to reference and pass down for years to come.

Scripture Reading Plan: The Romans reading plan is divided into daily readings with supplemental scriptures to help you understand the meaning and biblical context of the passage.

Response: Each daily reading in this Legacy Book closes with space for personal reflections and prayers.

Questions: Weekly discussion questions based on the certainty of the gospel are provided at the end of each week—perfect for small group gatherings or individual study.

Key Verse: The key verse of this Legacy Book, found on the facing page, represents the heart of the Romans reading plan.

Scripture Cards: Designed for memorization and sharing, the wallet-sized cards in the back of this Legacy Book display significant verses from the reading plan.

For additional guidance and supplemental reading, download the He Reads Truth™ mobile app from the iOS App Store.

For all have sinned and fall short of the glory of God. They are justified freely by his grace through the redemption that is in Christ Jesus.

ROMANS 3:23-24

Forbear to judge, for we are sinners all.

–HENRY VI, PART 2, III.iii

Welcome to our study of Paul's letter to the Romans.

Martin Luther said of this epistle, "It is well worth a Christian's while not only to memorize it word for word but also to occupy himself with it daily, as though it were the daily bread of the soul."

Why did Luther hold Romans in such high esteem? He said, "This letter is truly the most important piece in the New Testament. It is purest Gospel."

Strong words. What makes Romans so special? While all Scripture is God-breathed and equally valuable, Romans is unique. It is the most comprehensive, organized expression of Christian doctrine assembled in one place in the Bible.

Paul wrote this letter to explain to Jewish and Gentile converts what it meant to believe in and be redeemed by Jesus Christ. This book reaches back deep into the Old Testament. It walks us through the origin and problem of sin, the reality of guilt, the impossibility of saving ourselves, and the ultimate rescue we're given in the life, death, and resurrection of Jesus Christ.

Romans is meant to be thorough—a practical, theological guide for the follower of Jesus. Whether you are new to what it means to follow Christ, or have read this letter many times over, read this book as though it is telling a single story—the story of how God rescues us through the sacrifice of Christ.

Read on,

The He Reads Truth Team

Table of Contents

Grace to you and peace from God our Father and the Lord Jesus Christ.

ROMANS 1:7

Romans

AN INTRODUCTION

ON THE TIMELINE

The indisputable author of the book of Romans is the Apostle Paul. From the book of Acts and statements made in Romans, we learn that Paul wrote this letter while he was in Corinth in the spring of A.D. 57, while on his way to Jerusalem to deliver an offering from the Gentile churches to poor Jewish Christians (Acts 20:3; Romans 15:25-29). This places the writing of Romans at the end of Paul's third missionary journey.

A LITTLE BACKGROUND

The imposing city of Rome was the primary destination for this letter. Some manuscripts, however, lack the phrase "in Rome" (Romans 1:7), giving some support to the conclusion that Paul intended an even wider audience for the letter. The origin of the Roman house churches is unknown, though their foundations can be traced back to the "visitors from Rome, both Jews and proselytes" who came to Jerusalem at Pentecost (Acts 2:10), many of whom converted to Christianity (Acts 2:41).

MESSAGE & PURPOSE

Paul's letter to the Roman house churches has been a favorite among the New Testament writings for its theological and pastoral influence. It focuses on the doctrine of salvation, including the practical implications for believers as they live out the salvation given to them through Jesus Christ. Paul's purpose in writing the letter was to impart spiritual strength to the believers at Rome (Romans 1:11-12; 16:25-26). He asked for prayer for the difficult task he was undertaking (15:30-31) and that he might be able to visit them (15:32). Paul also hoped to enlist the Roman churches to support a mission to the west (15:23-29). In response to Jewish-Gentile tensions, Paul included an exposition of what is essential to Christianity and what are non-essentials.

GIVE THANKS FOR THE BOOK OF ROMANS

In the book of Romans, Paul emphasized righteousness and justification by grace through faith to a depth and detail not found elsewhere in the Bible. Paul also mapped out the spread of human sin and its results in both believers and nonbelievers. In Romans 6–8, Paul gave the most comprehensive development of our union with Christ and the Spirit's work in us.

Romans 1:1-17
2 Samuel 7:12-16
2 Corinthians 5:17

Set Apart for the Gospel

DATE

The Gospel Of God For Rome

[1] Paul, a servant of Christ Jesus, called as an apostle and set apart for the gospel of God— [2] which he promised beforehand through his prophets in the Holy Scriptures— [3] concerning his Son, Jesus Christ our Lord, who was a descendant of David according to the flesh [4] and was appointed to be the powerful Son of God according to the Spirit of holiness by the resurrection of the dead. [5] Through him we have received grace and apostleship to bring about the obedience of faith for the sake of his name among all the Gentiles, [6] including you who are also called by Jesus Christ.

[7] To all who are in Rome, loved by God, called as saints.

Grace to you and peace from God our Father and the Lord Jesus Christ.

Paul's Desire To Visit Rome

[8] First, I thank my God through Jesus Christ for all of you because the news of your faith is being reported in all the world. [9] God is my witness, whom I serve with my spirit in telling the good news about his Son—that I constantly mention you, [10] always asking in my prayers that if it is somehow in God's will, I may now at last succeed in coming to you. [11] For I want very much to see you, so that I may impart to you some spiritual gift to strengthen you, [12] that is, to be mutually encouraged by each other's faith, both yours and mine.

[13] Now I don't want you to be unaware, brothers and sisters, that I often planned to come to you (but was prevented until now) in order that I might have a fruitful ministry among you, just as I have had among the rest of the Gentiles. [14] I am obligated both to Greeks and barbarians, both to the wise and the foolish. [15] So I am eager to preach the gospel to you also who are in Rome.

The Righteous Will Live By Faith

[16] For I am not ashamed of the gospel, because it is the power of God for salvation to everyone who believes, first to the Jew, and also to the Greek. [17] For in it the righteousness of God is revealed from faith to faith, just as it is written: The righteous will live by faith.

2 SAMUEL 7:12-16

[12] "When your time comes and you rest with your fathers, I will raise up after you your descendant, who will come from your body, and I will establish his kingdom. [13] He is the one who will build a house for my name, and I will establish the throne of his kingdom forever. [14] I will be his father, and he will be my son. When he does wrong, I will discipline him with a rod of men and blows from mortals. [15] But my faithful love will never leave him as it did when I removed it from Saul, whom I removed from before you. [16] Your house and kingdom will endure before me forever, and your throne will be established forever."

2 CORINTHIANS 5:17

Therefore, if anyone is in Christ, he is a new creation; the old has passed away, and see, the new has come!

RESPONSE

Romans 1:18-32
Proverbs 1:7
2 Timothy 3:1-9

The Righteousness and Wrath of God

DATE

The Guilt Of The Gentile World

[18] For God's wrath is revealed from heaven against all godlessness and unrighteousness of people who by their unrighteousness suppress the truth, [19] since what can be known about God is evident among them, because God has shown it to them. [20] For his invisible attributes, that is, his eternal power and divine nature, have been clearly seen since the creation of the world, being understood through what he has made. As a result, people are without excuse. [21] For though they knew God, they did not glorify him as God or show gratitude. Instead, their thinking became worthless, and their senseless hearts were darkened. [22] Claiming to be wise, they became fools [23] and exchanged the glory of the immortal God for images resembling mortal man, birds, four-footed animals, and reptiles.

[24] Therefore God delivered them over in the desires of their hearts to sexual impurity, so that their bodies were degraded among themselves. [25] They exchanged the truth of God for a lie, and worshiped and served what has been created instead of the Creator, who is praised forever. Amen.

From Idolatry To Depravity

[26] For this reason God delivered them over to disgraceful passions. Their women exchanged natural sexual relations for unnatural ones. [27] The men in the same way also left natural relations with women and were inflamed in their lust for one another. Men committed shameless acts with men and received in their own persons the appropriate penalty of their error.

[28] And because they did not think it worthwhile to acknowledge God, God delivered them over to a corrupt mind so that they do what is not right. [29] They are filled with all unrighteousness, evil, greed, and wickedness. They are full of envy, murder, quarrels, deceit, and malice. They are gossips, [30] slanderers, God-haters, arrogant, proud, boastful, inventors of evil, disobedient to parents,

[31] senseless, untrustworthy, unloving, and unmerciful. [32] Although they know God's just sentence—that those who practice such things deserve to die—they not only do them, but even applaud others who practice them.

PROVERBS 1:7

The fear of the LORD
is the beginning of knowledge;
fools despise wisdom and discipline.

2 TIMOTHY 3:1-9

Difficult Times Ahead

[1] But know this: Hard times will come in the last days. [2] For people will be lovers of self, lovers of money, boastful, proud, demeaning, disobedient to parents, ungrateful, unholy, [3] unloving, irreconcilable, slanderers, without self-control, brutal, without love for what is good, [4] traitors, reckless, conceited, lovers of pleasure rather than lovers of God, [5] holding to the form of godliness but denying its power. Avoid these people.

[6] For among them are those who worm their way into households and deceive gullible women overwhelmed by sins and led astray by a variety of passions, [7] always learning and never able to come to a knowledge of the truth. [8] Just as Jannes and Jambres resisted Moses, so these also resist the truth. They are men who are corrupt in mind and worthless in regard to the faith. [9] But they will not make further progress, for their foolishness will be clear to all, as was the foolishness of Jannes and Jambres.

RESPONSE

Romans 2:1-16
Deuteronomy 16:18-20
Titus 1:15

Who Can Judge?

DATE _____

God's Righteous Judgment

[1] Therefore, every one of you who judges is without excuse. For when you judge another, you condemn yourself, since you, the judge, do the same things. [2] We know that God's judgment on those who do such things is based on the truth. [3] Do you really think—anyone of you who judges those who do such things yet do the same—that you will escape God's judgment? [4] Or do you despise the riches of his kindness, restraint, and patience, not recognizing that God's kindness is intended to lead you to repentance? [5] Because of your hardened and unrepentant heart you are storing up wrath for yourself in the day of wrath, when God's righteous judgment is revealed. [6] He will repay each one according to his works: [7] eternal life to those who by persistence in doing good seek glory, honor, and immortality; [8] but wrath and anger to those who are self-seeking and disobey the truth while obeying unrighteousness. [9] There will be affliction and distress for every human being who does evil, first to the Jew, and also to the Greek; [10] but glory, honor, and peace for everyone who does what is good, first to the Jew, and also to the Greek. [11] For there is no favoritism with God.

[12] All who sin without the law will also perish without the law, and all who sin under the law will be judged by the law. [13] For the hearers of the law are not righteous before God, but the doers of the law will be justified. [14] So, when Gentiles, who do not by nature have the law, do what the law demands, they are a law to themselves even though they do not have the law. [15] They show that the work of the law is written on their hearts. Their consciences confirm this. Their competing thoughts either accuse or even excuse them [16] on the day when God judges what people have kept secret, according to my gospel through Christ Jesus.

Appointing Judges And Officials

[18] Appoint judges and officials for your tribes in all your towns the LORD your God is giving you. They are to judge the people with righteous judgment. [19] Do not deny justice or show partiality to anyone. Do not accept a bribe, for it blinds the eyes of the wise and twists the words of the righteous. [20] Pursue justice and justice alone, so that you will live and possess the land the LORD your God is giving you.

To the pure, everything is pure, but to those who are defiled and unbelieving nothing is pure; in fact, both their mind and conscience are defiled.

RESPONSE

Romans 2:17-29
Deuteronomy 7:25-26
Psalm 51:1-12

The Spirit of the Law

DATE _____

Jewish Violation Of The Law

[17] Now if you call yourself a Jew, and rely on the law, and boast in God, [18] and know his will, and approve the things that are superior, being instructed from the law, [19] and if you are convinced that you are a guide for the blind, a light to those in darkness, [20] an instructor of the ignorant, a teacher of the immature, having the embodiment of knowledge and truth in the law— [21] you then, who teach another, don't you teach yourself? You who preach, "You must not steal"—do you steal? [22] You who say, "You must not commit adultery"—do you commit adultery? You who detest idols, do you rob their temples? [23] You who boast in the law, do you dishonor God by breaking the law? [24] For, as it is written: The name of God is blasphemed among the Gentiles because of you.

Circumcision Of The Heart

[25] Circumcision benefits you if you observe the law, but if you are a lawbreaker, your circumcision has become uncircumcision. [26] So if an uncircumcised man keeps the law's requirements, will not his uncircumcision be counted as circumcision? [27] A man who is physically uncircumcised, but who keeps the law, will judge you who are a lawbreaker in spite of having the letter of the law and circumcision. [28] For a person is not a Jew who is one outwardly, and true circumcision is not something visible in the flesh. [29] On the contrary, a person is a Jew who is one inwardly, and circumcision is of the heart—by the Spirit, not the letter. That person's praise is not from people but from God.

[25] Burn up the carved images of their gods. Don't covet the silver and gold on the images and take it for yourself, or else you will be ensnared by it, for it is detestable to the LORD your God. [26] Do not bring any detestable thing into your house, or you will be set apart for destruction like it. You are to abhor and detest it utterly because it is set apart for destruction.

A Prayer For Restoration

For the choir director. A psalm of David, when the prophet
Nathan came to him after he had gone to Bathsheba.

¹ Be gracious to me, God,

according to your faithful love;

according to your abundant compassion,

blot out my rebellion.

² Completely wash away my guilt

and cleanse me from my sin.

³ For I am conscious of my rebellion,

and my sin is always before me.

⁴ Against you—you alone—I have sinned

and done this evil in your sight.

So you are right when you pass sentence;

you are blameless when you judge.

⁵ Indeed, I was guilty when I was born;

I was sinful when my mother conceived me.

⁶ Surely you desire integrity in the inner self,

and you teach me wisdom deep within.

⁷ Purify me with hyssop, and I will be clean;

wash me, and I will be whiter than snow.

⁸ Let me hear joy and gladness;

let the bones you have crushed rejoice.

⁹ Turn your face away from my sins

and blot out all my guilt.

¹⁰ God, create a clean heart for me

and renew a steadfast spirit within me.

¹¹ Do not banish me from your presence
or take your Holy Spirit from me.
¹² Restore the joy of your salvation to me,
and sustain me by giving me a willing spirit.

RESPONSE

Romans 3:1-20
Psalm 14
Ecclesiastes 7:20

Guilty as Charged

DATE _____

Paul Answers An Objection

[1] So what advantage does the Jew have? Or what is the benefit of circumcision? [2] Considerable in every way. First, they were entrusted with the very words of God. [3] What then? If some were unfaithful, will their unfaithfulness nullify God's faithfulness? [4] Absolutely not! Let God be true, even though everyone is a liar, as it is written:

> That you may be justified in your words
> and triumph when you judge.

[5] But if our unrighteousness highlights God's righteousness, what are we to say? I am using a human argument: Is God unrighteous to inflict wrath? [6] Absolutely not! Otherwise, how will God judge the world? [7] But if by my lie God's truth abounds to his glory, why am I also still being judged as a sinner? [8] And why not say, just as some people slanderously claim we say, "Let us do what is evil so that good may come"? Their condemnation is deserved!

The Whole World Guilty Before God

[9] What then? Are we any better off? Not at all! For we have already charged that both Jews and Gentiles are all under sin, [10] as it is written:

> There is no one righteous, not even one.
> [11] There is no one who understands;
> there is no one who seeks God.
> [12] All have turned away;
> all alike have become worthless.
> There is no one who does what is good,
> not even one.
> [13] Their throat is an open grave;
> they deceive with their tongues.
> Vipers' venom is under their lips.
> [14] Their mouth is full of cursing and bitterness.

¹⁵ Their feet are swift to shed blood;

¹⁶ ruin and wretchedness are in their paths,

¹⁷ and the path of peace they have not known.

¹⁸ There is no fear of God before their eyes.

¹⁹ Now we know that whatever the law says, it speaks to those who are subject to the law, so that every mouth may be shut and the whole world may become subject to God's judgment. ²⁰ For no one will be justified in his sight by the works of the law, because the knowledge of sin comes through the law.

PSALM 14

A Portrait Of Sinners

For the choir director. Of David.

¹ The fool says in his heart, "There's no God."
They are corrupt; they do vile deeds.
There is no one who does good.
² The Lord looks down from heaven on the human race
to see if there is one who is wise,
one who seeks God.
³ All have turned away;
all alike have become corrupt.
There is no one who does good,
not even one.

⁴ Will evildoers never understand?
They consume my people as they consume bread;
they do not call on the Lord.

⁵ Then they will be filled with dread,
for God is with those who are righteous.
⁶ You sinners frustrate the plans of the oppressed,
but the LORD is his refuge.

⁷ Oh, that Israel's deliverance would come from Zion!
When the LORD restores the fortunes of his people,
let Jacob rejoice, let Israel be glad.

ECCLESIASTES 7:20

There is certainly no one righteous on the earth
who does good and never sins.

RESPONSE

RESPONSE

Grace Day

Take this day as an opportunity to catch up on your reading, pray, and rest in the presence of the Lord. If you'd like, play or sing this hymn inspired by the book of Romans.

Psalm 51:1-3

¹ Be gracious to me, God,
according to your faithful love;
according to your abundant compassion,
blot out my rebellion.
² Completely wash away my guilt
and cleanse me from my sin.
³ For I am conscious of my rebellion,
and my sin is always before me.

DATE

AMAZING GRACE

ROMANS 5:1-5

1 A - maz - ing grace— how sweet the sound—
2 'Twas grace that taught my heart to fear,
3 The Lord has prom - ised good to me,
4 Through man - y dan - gers, toils, and snares
5 When we've been there ten thou - sand years,

that saved a wretch like me! I once was lost
and grace my fears re - lieved; how pre - cious did
His word my hope se - cures; He will my shield
I have al - read - y come; 'tis grace hath brought
bright shin - ing as the sun, we've no less days

but now am found, was blind but now I see.
that grace ap - pear the hour I first be - lieved!
and por - tion be as long as life en - dures.
me safe thus far, and grace will lead me home.
to sing God's praise than when we'd first be - gun.

Text: John Newton, 1779 | Tune: Virginia Harmony, 1831

Discussion Questions

The book of Romans is a thorough and succinct presentation of the message of Jesus Christ—the essential gospel. In chapter 8, Paul asks a series of open-ended questions which help us consider the effect of this gospel in the life of a believer. Each week we will return to this passage and this string of questions to explore what each one means and how to apply them.

Read Romans 8:18-39 and discuss the following questions as a group, or use them as journaling prompts to work and pray through on your own.

WHAT THEN ARE WE TO SAY ABOUT THESE THINGS?

ROMANS 8:31

I What is the context that comes right before this question is asked? What are "these things"?

II What is the context that follows immediately after this question? What does Paul say about "these things"? How does he answer his own question?

III Scriptural truth demands we give a response. It is personal; we have to do something with it. What are some of the major questions and declarations the gospel calls us to respond to? Try to name at least three.

Weekly Truth

Memorizing Scripture is a way to carry God's Word with you wherever you go, keeping God-breathed instruction, reproof, and truth in your heart and mind each day.

As we read through Romans together, we will memorize the steps in the Romans Road to salvation, a concise explanation of the gospel using verses from this epistle. The first step acknowledges the **problem:** our own sin.

Romans 3:23 | For all have sinned and fall short of the glory of God.

DATE

NOTES

Romans 3:21-31
Ephesians 1:7-10
Colossians 1:13-14

Faith Upholds the Law

DATE

The Righteousness Of God Through Faith

²¹ But now, apart from the law, the righteousness of God has been revealed, attested by the Law and the Prophets. ²² The righteousness of God is through faith in Jesus Christ to all who believe, since there is no distinction. ²³ For all have sinned and fall short of the glory of God. ²⁴ They are justified freely by his grace through the redemption that is in Christ Jesus. ²⁵ God presented him as an atoning sacrifice in his blood, received through faith, to demonstrate his righteousness, because in his restraint God passed over the sins previously committed. ²⁶ God presented him to demonstrate his righteousness at the present time, so that he would be righteous and declare righteous the one who has faith in Jesus.

Boasting Excluded

²⁷ Where, then, is boasting? It is excluded. By what kind of law? By one of works? No, on the contrary, by a law of faith. ²⁸ For we conclude that a person is justified by faith apart from the works of the law. ²⁹ Or is God the God of Jews only? Is he not the God of Gentiles too? Yes, of Gentiles too, ³⁰ since there is one God who will justify the circumcised by faith and the uncircumcised through faith. ³¹ Do we then nullify the law through faith? Absolutely not! On the contrary, we uphold the law.

⁷ In him we have redemption through his blood, the forgiveness of our trespasses, according to the riches of his grace ⁸ that he richly poured out on us with all wisdom and understanding. ⁹ He made known to us the mystery of his will, according to his good pleasure that he purposed in Christ ¹⁰ as a plan for the right time—to bring everything together in Christ, both things in heaven and things on earth in him.

[13] He has rescued us from the domain of darkness and transferred us into the kingdom of the Son he loves. [14] In him we have redemption, the forgiveness of sins.

RESPONSE

DAY 9

Romans 4
Psalm 32:1-2
Ephesians 2:4-7

The Promise Granted through Faith

DATE _____

ROMANS 4

Abraham Justified By Faith

[1] What then will we say that Abraham, our forefather according to the flesh, has found? [2] If Abraham was justified by works, he has something to boast about—but not before God. [3] For what does the Scripture say? Abraham believed God, and it was credited to him for righteousness. [4] Now to the one who works, pay is not credited as a gift, but as something owed. [5] But to the one who does not work, but believes on him who declares the ungodly to be righteous, his faith is credited for righteousness.

David Celebrating The Same Truth

[6] Just as David also speaks of the blessing of the person to whom God credits righteousness apart from works:

[7] Blessed are those whose lawless acts are forgiven
and whose sins are covered.
[8] Blessed is the person
the Lord will never charge with sin.

Abraham Justified Before Circumcision

[9] Is this blessing only for the circumcised, then? Or is it also for the uncircumcised? For we say, Faith was credited to Abraham for righteousness. [10] In what way then was it credited—while he was circumcised, or uncircumcised? It was not while he was circumcised, but uncircumcised. [11] And he received the sign of circumcision as a seal of the righteousness that he had by faith while still uncircumcised. This was to make him the father of all who believe but are not circumcised, so that righteousness may be credited to them also. [12] And he became the father of the circumcised, who are not only circumcised but who also follow in the footsteps of the faith our father Abraham had while he was still uncircumcised.

The Promise Granted Through Faith

¹³ For the promise to Abraham or to his descendants that he would inherit the world was not through the law, but through the righteousness that comes by faith. ¹⁴ If those who are of the law are heirs, faith is made empty and the promise nullified, ¹⁵ because the law produces wrath. And where there is no law, there is no transgression.

¹⁶ This is why the promise is by faith, so that it may be according to grace, to guarantee it to all the descendants—not only to those who are of the law but also to those who are of Abraham's faith. He is the father of us all. ¹⁷ As it is written: I have made you the father of many nations. He is our father in God's sight, in whom Abraham believed—the God who gives life to the dead and calls things into existence that do not exist. ¹⁸ He believed, hoping against hope, so that he became the father of many nations according to what had been spoken: So will your descendants be. ¹⁹ He did not weaken in faith when he considered his own body to be already dead (since he was about a hundred years old) and also the deadness of Sarah's womb. ²⁰ He did not waver in unbelief at God's promise but was strengthened in his faith and gave glory to God, ²¹ because he was fully convinced that what God had promised, he was also able to do. ²² Therefore, it was credited to him for righteousness. ²³ Now it was credited to him was not written for Abraham alone, ²⁴ but also for us. It will be credited to us who believe in him who raised Jesus our Lord from the dead. ²⁵ He was delivered up for our trespasses and raised for our justification.

PSALM 32:1-2

¹How joyful is the one
whose transgression is forgiven,
whose sin is covered!
² How joyful is a person whom
the Lord does not charge with iniquity
and in whose spirit is no deceit!

⁴ But God, who is rich in mercy, because of his great love that he had for us, ⁵ made us alive with Christ even though we were dead in trespasses. You are saved by grace! ⁶ He also raised us up with him and seated us with him in the heavens in Christ Jesus, ⁷ so that in the coming ages he might display the immeasurable riches of his grace through his kindness to us in Christ Jesus.

RESPONSE

RESPONSE

Romans 5:1-11
Galatians 4:6-7
Ephesians 2:18-22

A Hope That Will Not Disappoint

DATE

Faith Triumphs

[1] Therefore, since we have been declared righteous by faith, we have peace with God through our Lord Jesus Christ. [2] We have also obtained access through him by faith into this grace in which we stand, and we rejoice in the hope of the glory of God. [3] And not only that, but we also rejoice in our afflictions, because we know that affliction produces endurance, [4] endurance produces proven character, and proven character produces hope. [5] This hope will not disappoint us, because God's love has been poured out in our hearts through the Holy Spirit who was given to us.

Those Declared Righteous Are Reconciled

[6] For while we were still helpless, at the right time, Christ died for the ungodly. [7] For rarely will someone die for a just person—though for a good person perhaps someone might even dare to die. [8] But God proves his own love for us in that while we were still sinners, Christ died for us. [9] How much more then, since we have now been declared righteous by his blood, will we be saved through him from wrath. [10] For if, while we were enemies, we were reconciled to God through the death of his Son, then how much more, having been reconciled, will we be saved by his life. [11] And not only that, but we also rejoice in God through our Lord Jesus Christ, through whom we have now received this reconciliation.

[6] And because you are sons, God sent the Spirit of his Son into our hearts, crying, "Abba, Father!" [7] So you are no longer a slave but a son, and if a son, then God has made you an heir.

[18] For through him we both have access in one spirit to the Father. [19] So then you are no longer foreigners and strangers, but fellow citizens with the saints, and members of God's household, [20] built on the foundation of the apostles and prophets, with Christ Jesus himself as the cornerstone. [21] In him the whole building, being put together, grows into a holy temple in the Lord. [22] In him you are also being built together for God's dwelling in the Spirit.

RESPONSE

Romans 5:12-21
1 Corinthians 15:21-22
Genesis 3:17-19

Death through Adam and Life through Christ

DATE

Death Through Adam And Life Through Christ

[12] Therefore, just as sin entered the world through one man, and death through sin, in this way death spread to all people, because all sinned. [13] In fact, sin was in the world before the law, but sin is not charged to a person's account when there is no law. [14] Nevertheless, death reigned from Adam to Moses, even over those who did not sin in the likeness of Adam's transgression. He is a type of the Coming One.

[15] But the gift is not like the trespass. For if by the one man's trespass the many died, how much more have the grace of God and the gift which comes through the grace of the one man Jesus Christ overflowed to the many. [16] And the gift is not like the one man's sin, because from one sin came the judgment, resulting in condemnation, but from many trespasses came the gift, resulting in justification. [17] Since by the one man's trespass, death reigned through that one man, how much more will those who receive the overflow of grace and the gift of righteousness reign in life through the one man, Jesus Christ.

[18] So then, as through one trespass there is condemnation for everyone, so also through one righteous act there is justification leading to life for everyone. [19] For just as through one man's disobedience the many were made sinners, so also through the one man's obedience the many will be made righteous. [20] The law came along to multiply the trespass. But where sin multiplied, grace multiplied even more [21] so that, just as sin reigned in death, so also grace will reign through righteousness, resulting in eternal life through Jesus Christ our Lord.

[21] For since death came through a man, the resurrection of the dead also comes through a man. [22] For just as in Adam all die, so also in Christ all will be made alive.

[17] And he said to the man, "Because you listened to your wife and ate from the tree about which I commanded you, 'Do not eat from it':

> The ground is cursed because of you.
> You will eat from it by means of painful labor
> all the days of your life.
> [18] It will produce thorns and thistles for you,
> and you will eat the plants of the field.
> [19] You will eat bread by the sweat of your brow
> until you return to the ground,
> since you were taken from it.
> For you are dust,
> and you will return to dust."

RESPONSE

Romans 6:1-14
2 Corinthians 5:18-21
Colossians 3:1-11

Our New Life in Christ

DATE _____

The New Life In Christ

[1] What should we say then? Should we continue in sin so that grace may multiply? [2] Absolutely not! How can we who died to sin still live in it? [3] Or are you unaware that all of us who were baptized into Christ Jesus were baptized into his death? [4] Therefore we were buried with him by baptism into death, in order that, just as Christ was raised from the dead by the glory of the Father, so we too may walk in newness of life. [5] For if we have been united with him in the likeness of his death, we will certainly also be in the likeness of his resurrection. [6] For we know that our old self was crucified with him so that the body ruled by sin might be rendered powerless so that we may no longer be enslaved to sin, [7] since a person who has died is freed from sin. [8] Now if we died with Christ, we believe that we will also live with him, [9] because we know that Christ, having been raised from the dead, will not die again. Death no longer rules over him. [10] For the death he died, he died to sin once for all time; but the life he lives, he lives to God. [11] So, you too consider yourselves dead to sin and alive to God in Christ Jesus.

[12] Therefore do not let sin reign in your mortal body, so that you obey its desires. [13] And do not offer any parts of it to sin as weapons for unrighteousness. But as those who are alive from the dead, offer yourselves to God, and all the parts of yourselves to God as weapons for righteousness. [14] For sin will not rule over you, because you are not under the law but under grace.

2 CORINTHIANS 5:18-21

[18] Everything is from God, who has reconciled us to himself through Christ and has given us the ministry of reconciliation. [19] That is, in Christ, God was reconciling the world to himself, not counting their trespasses against them, and he has committed the message of reconciliation to us.

²⁰ Therefore, we are ambassadors for Christ, since God is making his appeal through us. We plead on Christ's behalf: "Be reconciled to God." ²¹ He made the one who did not know sin to be sin for us, so that in him we might become the righteousness of God.

COLOSSIANS 3:1-11

The Life Of The New Man

¹ So if you have been raised with Christ, seek the things above, where Christ is, seated at the right hand of God. ² Set your minds on things above, not on earthly things. ³ For you died, and your life is hidden with Christ in God. ⁴ When Christ, who is your life, appears, then you also will appear with him in glory.

⁵ Therefore, put to death what belongs to your earthly nature: sexual immorality, impurity, lust, evil desire, and greed, which is idolatry. ⁶ Because of these, God's wrath is coming upon the disobedient, ⁷ and you once walked in these things when you were living in them. ⁸ But now, put away all the following: anger, wrath, malice, slander, and filthy language from your mouth. ⁹ Do not lie to one another, since you have put off the old self with its practices ¹⁰ and have put on the new self. You are being renewed in knowledge according to the image of your Creator. ¹¹ In Christ there is not Greek and Jew, circumcision and uncircumcision, barbarian, Scythian, slave and free; but Christ is all and in all.

RESPONSE

Grace Day

Take this day as an opportunity to catch up on your reading, pray, and rest in the presence of the Lord. If you'd like, play or sing this hymn inspired by the book of Romans.

Colossians
1:13-14

He has rescued us from the domain of darkness and transferred us into the kingdom of the Son he loves. In him we have redemption, the forgiveness of sins.

DATE

ROCK OF AGES, CLEFT FOR ME

ROMANS 6:17-23

Text: Augustus M. Toplady, 1776 | Tune: Thomas Hastings, 1830

Discussion Questions

The book of Romans is a thorough and succinct presentation of the message of Jesus Christ—the essential gospel. In chapter 8, Paul asks a series of open-ended questions which help us consider the effect of this gospel in the life of a believer. Each week we will return to this passage and this string of questions to explore what each one means and how to apply them.

Read Romans 8:18-39 and discuss the following questions as a group, or use them as journaling prompts to work and pray through on your own.

IF GOD IS FOR US, WHO IS AGAINST US?

ROMANS 8:31

I   This little verse makes a big statement. What are some ways we might underestimate what is being said here? What are some ways we might take this verse out of context?

II   Who or what do you most often feel is against you? Why?

III   In what ways is God for us? Try to name at least three distinct ways.

Weekly Truth

Memorizing Scripture is a way to carry God's Word with you wherever you go, keeping God-breathed instruction, reproof, and truth in your heart and mind each day.

As we read through Romans together, we are memorizing the steps in the Romans Road to salvation. The second step recognizes the **consequence** *of our sin: death.*

Romans 6:23

For the wages of sin is death, but the gift of God is eternal life in Christ Jesus our Lord.

DATE

NOTES

Romans 6:15-23
Galatians 5:13-14
1 Peter 2:11-17

From Slaves of Sin to Slaves of God

DATE

From Slaves Of Sin To Slaves Of God

[15] What then? Should we sin because we are not under the law but under grace? Absolutely not! [16] Don't you know that if you offer yourselves to someone as obedient slaves, you are slaves of that one you obey—either of sin leading to death or of obedience leading to righteousness? [17] But thank God that, although you used to be slaves of sin, you obeyed from the heart that pattern of teaching to which you were handed over, [18] and having been set free from sin, you became enslaved to righteousness. [19] I am using a human analogy because of the weakness of your flesh. For just as you offered the parts of yourselves as slaves to impurity, and to greater and greater lawlessness, so now offer them as slaves to righteousness, which results in sanctification. [20] For when you were slaves of sin, you were free with regard to righteousness. [21] So what fruit was produced then from the things you are now ashamed of? The outcome of those things is death. [22] But now, since you have been set free from sin and have become enslaved to God, you have your fruit, which results in sanctification— and the outcome is eternal life! [23] For the wages of sin is death, but the gift of God is eternal life in Christ Jesus our Lord.

[13] For you were called to be free, brothers and sisters; only don't use this freedom as an opportunity for the flesh, but serve one another through love. [14] For the whole law is fulfilled in one statement: Love your neighbor as yourself.

A Call To Good Works

[11] Dear friends, I urge you as strangers and exiles to abstain from sinful desires that wage war against the soul. [12] Conduct yourselves honorably among the Gentiles, so that when they slander you as evildoers, they will observe your good works and will glorify God on the day he visits.

[13] Submit to every human authority because of the Lord, whether to the emperor as the supreme authority [14] or to governors as those sent out by him to punish those who do what is evil and to praise those who do what is good. [15] For it is God's will that you silence the ignorance of foolish people by doing good. [16] Submit as free people, not using your freedom as a cover-up for evil, but as God's slaves. [17] Honor everyone. Love the brothers and sisters. Fear God. Honor the emperor.

RESPONSE

Romans 7:1-13
Proverbs 1:19
John 14:6-7

How Can
Death Bring
Life?

DATE

An Illustration From Marriage

[1] Since I am speaking to those who know the law, brothers and sisters, don't you know that the law rules over someone as long as he lives? [2] For example, a married woman is legally bound to her husband while he lives. But if her husband dies, she is released from the law regarding the husband. [3] So then, if she is married to another man while her husband is living, she will be called an adulteress. But if her husband dies, she is free from that law. Then, if she is married to another man, she is not an adulteress.

[4] Therefore, my brothers and sisters, you also were put to death in relation to the law through the body of Christ so that you may belong to another. You belong to him who was raised from the dead in order that we may bear fruit for God. [5] For when we were in the flesh, the sinful passions aroused through the law were working in us to bear fruit for death. [6] But now we have been released from the law, since we have died to what held us, so that we may serve in the newness of the Spirit and not in the old letter of the law.

Sin's Use Of The Law

[7] What should we say then? Is the law sin? Absolutely not! On the contrary, I would not have known sin if it were not for the law. For example, I would not have known what it is to covet if the law had not said, Do not covet. [8] And sin, seizing an opportunity through the commandment, produced in me coveting of every kind. For apart from the law sin is dead. [9] Once I was alive apart from the law, but when the commandment came, sin sprang to life again [10] and I died. The commandment that was meant for life resulted in death for me. [11] For sin, seizing an opportunity through the commandment, deceived me, and through it killed me. [12] So then, the law is holy, and the commandment is holy and just and good. [13] Therefore, did what is good become death to me? Absolutely not! On the contrary, sin, in order to be recognized as sin, was producing death in me through what is good, so that through the commandment, sin might become sinful beyond measure.

PROVERBS 1:19

Such are the paths of all who make profit dishonestly;
it takes the lives of those who receive it.

JOHN 14:6-7

[6] Jesus told him, "I am the way, the truth, and the life. No one comes to the Father except through me. [7] If you know me, you will also know my Father. From now on you do know him and have seen him."

RESPONSE

HE READS TRUTH   75

Romans 7:14-25
Galatians 5:16-26
1 John 1:8-10

The Good
I Want to Do

DATE _____

The Problem Of Sin In Us

[14] For we know that the law is spiritual, but I am of the flesh, sold as a slave to sin. [15] For I do not understand what I am doing, because I do not practice what I want to do, but I do what I hate. [16] Now if I do what I do not want to do, I agree with the law that it is good. [17] So now I am no longer the one doing it, but it is sin living in me. [18] For I know that nothing good lives in me, that is, in my flesh. For the desire to do what is good is with me, but there is no ability to do it. [19] For I do not do the good that I want to do, but I practice the evil that I do not want to do. [20] Now if I do what I do not want, I am no longer the one that does it, but it is the sin that lives in me. [21] So I discover this law: When I want to do what is good, evil is present with me. [22] For in my inner self I delight in God's law, [23] but I see a different law in the parts of my body, waging war against the law of my mind and taking me prisoner to the law of sin in the parts of my body. [24] What a wretched man I am! Who will rescue me from this body of death? [25] Thanks be to God through Jesus Christ our Lord! So then, with my mind I myself am serving the law of God, but with my flesh, the law of sin.

The Spirit Versus The Flesh

[16] I say then, walk by the Spirit and you will certainly not carry out the desire of the flesh. [17] For the flesh desires what is against the Spirit, and the Spirit desires what is against the flesh; these are opposed to each other, so that you don't do what you want. [18] But if you are led by the Spirit, you are not under the law.

[19] Now the works of the flesh are obvious: sexual immorality, moral impurity, promiscuity, [20] idolatry, sorcery, hatreds, strife, jealousy, outbursts of anger, selfish ambitions, dissensions, factions, [21] envy, drunkenness, carousing, and anything similar. I am warning you about these things—as I warned you before—that those who practice such things will not inherit the kingdom of God.

²² But the fruit of the Spirit is love, joy, peace, patience, kindness, goodness, faithfulness, ²³ gentleness, and self-control. The law is not against such things. ²⁴ Now those who belong to Christ Jesus have crucified the flesh with its passions and desires. ²⁵ If we live by the Spirit, let us also keep in step with the Spirit. ²⁶ Let us not become conceited, provoking one another, envying one another.

1 JOHN 1:8-10

⁸ If we say, "We have no sin," we are deceiving ourselves, and the truth is not in us. ⁹ If we confess our sins, he is faithful and righteous to forgive us our sins and to cleanse us from all unrighteousness. ¹⁰ If we say, "We have not sinned," we make him a liar, and his word is not in us.

RESPONSE

Romans 8:1-17
Isaiah 53:10
Mark 14:32-36

Joint Heirs
with Christ

DATE

The Life-Giving Spirit

[1] Therefore, there is now no condemnation for those in Christ Jesus, [2] because the law of the Spirit of life in Christ Jesus has set you free from the law of sin and death. [3] What the law could not do since it was weakened by the flesh, God did. He condemned sin in the flesh by sending his own Son in the likeness of sinful flesh as a sin offering, [4] in order that the law's requirement would be fulfilled in us who do not walk according to the flesh but according to the Spirit. [5] For those who live according to the flesh have their minds set on the things of the flesh, but those who live according to the Spirit have their minds set on the things of the Spirit. [6] Now the mindset of the flesh is death, but the mindset of the Spirit is life and peace. [7] The mindset of the flesh is hostile to God because it does not submit to God's law. Indeed, it is unable to do so. [8] Those who are in the flesh cannot please God. [9] You, however, are not in the flesh, but in the Spirit, if indeed the Spirit of God lives in you. If anyone does not have the Spirit of Christ, he does not belong to him. [10] Now if Christ is in you, the body is dead because of sin, but the Spirit gives life because of righteousness. [11] And if the Spirit of him who raised Jesus from the dead lives in you, then he who raised Christ from the dead will also bring your mortal bodies to life through his Spirit who lives in you.

The Holy Spirit's Ministries

[12] So then, brothers and sisters, we are not obligated to the flesh to live according to the flesh, [13] because if you live according to the flesh, you are going to die. But if by the Spirit you put to death the deeds of the body, you will live. [14] For all those led by God's Spirit are God's sons. [15] You did not receive a spirit of slavery to fall back into fear. Instead, you received the Spirit of adoption, by whom we cry out, "Abba, Father!" [16] The Spirit himself testifies together with our spirit that we are God's children, [17] and if children, also heirs—heirs of God and coheirs with Christ—if indeed we suffer with him so that we may also be glorified with him.

Yet the LORD was pleased to crush him severely.

When you make him a guilt offering,

he will see his seed, he will prolong his days,

and by his hand, the LORD's pleasure will be accomplished.

MARK 14:32-36

[32] Then they came to a place named Gethsemane, and he told his disciples, "Sit here while I pray." [33] He took Peter, James, and John with him, and he began to be deeply distressed and troubled. [34] He said to them, "I am deeply grieved to the point of death. Remain here and stay awake." [35] He went a little farther, fell to the ground, and prayed that if it were possible, the hour might pass from him. [36] And he said, "Abba, Father! All things are possible for you. Take this cup away from me. Nevertheless, not what I will, but what you will."

RESPONSE

From Groans to Glory

DATE _____

From Groans To Glory

[18] For I consider that the sufferings of this present time are not worth comparing with the glory that is going to be revealed to us. [19] For the creation eagerly waits with anticipation for God's sons to be revealed. [20] For the creation was subjected to futility—not willingly, but because of him who subjected it—in the hope [21] that the creation itself will also be set free from the bondage to decay into the glorious freedom of God's children. [22] For we know that the whole creation has been groaning together with labor pains until now. [23] Not only that, but we ourselves who have the Spirit as the firstfruits—we also groan within ourselves, eagerly waiting for adoption, the redemption of our bodies. [24] Now in this hope we were saved, but hope that is seen is not hope, because who hopes for what he sees? [25] Now if we hope for what we do not see, we eagerly wait for it with patience.

"For I will create a new heaven and a new earth;
the past events will not be remembered or come to mind."

The Comfort Of Christ's Coming

[13] We do not want you to be uninformed, brothers and sisters, concerning those who are asleep, so that you will not grieve like the rest, who have no hope. [14] For if we believe that Jesus died and rose again, in the same way, through Jesus, God will bring with him those who have fallen asleep. [15] For we say this to you by a word from the Lord: We who are still alive at the Lord's coming will certainly not precede those who have fallen asleep. [16] For the Lord himself will descend from heaven with a shout, with the archangel's voice, and with the trumpet of God, and the dead in Christ will rise first. [17] Then we who

are still alive, who are left, will be caught up together with them in the clouds to meet the Lord in the air, and so we will always be with the Lord. [18] Therefore encourage one another with these words.

REVELATION 21:1-6

The New Creation

[1] Then I saw a new heaven and a new earth; for the first heaven and the first earth had passed away, and the sea was no more. [2] I also saw the holy city, the new Jerusalem, coming down out of heaven from God, prepared like a bride adorned for her husband.

[3] Then I heard a loud voice from the throne: Look, God's dwelling is with humanity, and he will live with them. They will be his peoples, and God himself will be with them and will be their God. [4] He will wipe away every tear from their eyes. Death will be no more; grief, crying, and pain will be no more, because the previous things have passed away.

[5] Then the one seated on the throne said, "Look, I am making everything new." He also said, "Write, because these words are faithful and true." [6] Then he said to me, "It is done! I am the Alpha and the Omega, the beginning and the end. I will freely give to the thirsty from the spring of the water of life."

RESPONSE

Grace Day

Take this day as an opportunity to catch up on your reading, pray, and rest in the presence of the Lord. If you'd like, play or sing this hymn inspired by the book of Romans.

Galatians 5:13 | For you were called to be free, brothers and sisters; only don't use this freedom as an opportunity for the flesh, but serve one another through love.

DATE

AND CAN IT BE THAT I SHOULD GAIN?

ROMANS 8:1

Text: Charles Wesley 1738 | Tune: Thomas Campbell 1825

Discussion Questions

The book of Romans is a thorough and succinct presentation of the message of Jesus Christ–the essential gospel. In chapter 8, Paul asks a series of open-ended questions which help us consider the effect of this gospel in the life of a believer. Each week we will return to this passage and this string of questions to explore what each one means and how to apply them.

Read Romans 8:18-39 and discuss the following questions as a group, or use them as journaling prompts to work and pray through on your own.

HE DID NOT EVEN SPARE HIS OWN SON BUT OFFERED HIM UP FOR US ALL. HOW WILL HE NOT ALSO WITH HIM GRANT US EVERYTHING?

ROMANS 8:32

How would you put this verse into your own words? What is this verse saying?

 What are some of the things God will give us because He has also given us Christ? Are there things you feel you need that sometimes seem more important than what God has given you in Christ?

III How long do God's promises stand? In what timeframe do you tend to view God's promises? Why do we struggle to see things through the lens of eternity?

Weekly Truth

Memorizing Scripture is a way to carry God's Word with you wherever you go, keeping God-breathed instruction, reproof, and truth in your heart and mind each day.

As we read through Romans together, we are memorizing the steps in the Romans Road to salvation. The third step presents the **solution** to our problem: Jesus.

Romans 5:8

But God proves his own love for us in that while we were still sinners, Christ died for us.

DATE

NOTES

NOTES

EXTRAS

THE RISE OF THE ROMAN EMPIRE AND THE SPREAD OF CHRISTIANITY

This map shows the reach of the Roman Empire in four phases.

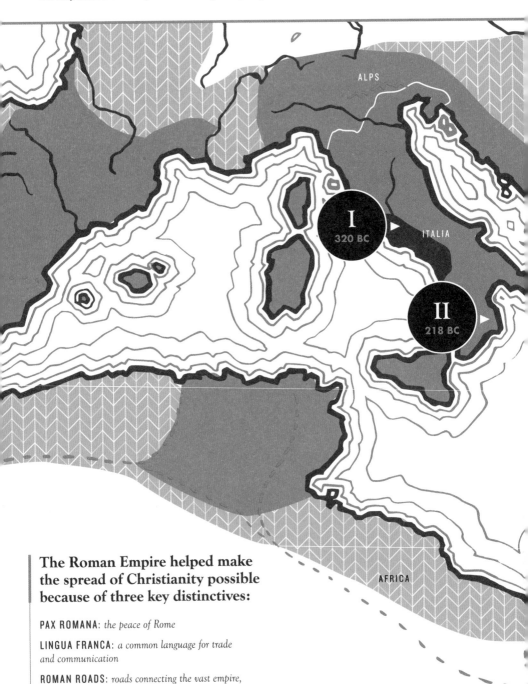

ALPS

I
320 BC

ITALIA

II
218 BC

AFRICA

The Roman Empire helped make the spread of Christianity possible because of three key distinctives:

PAX ROMANA: *the peace of Rome*

LINGUA FRANCA: *a common language for trade and communication*

ROMAN ROADS: *roads connecting the vast empire, facilitating safe travel*

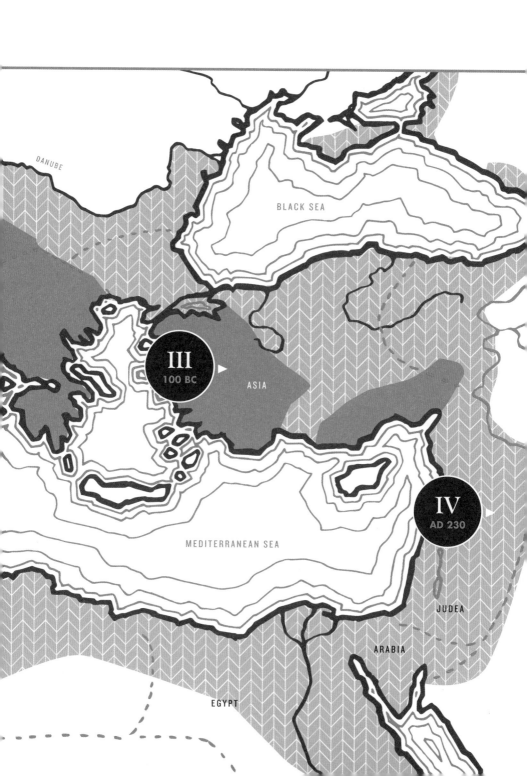

DANUBE

BLACK SEA

ASIA

III
100 BC

IV
AD 230

MEDITERRANEAN SEA

JUDEA

ARABIA

EGYPT

Roman Numerals

Roman Numerals originated in ancient Rome as a simple way to tally money and property, and remained in common use until the late medieval period. Even today we continue to use them in outlines, major sporting events, movie production dates, and world wars. In modern usage, Roman Numerals emphasize gravitas and importance.

THE ROMAN NUMERAL SYSTEM IS WRITTEN USING ONLY SEVEN UNIQUE SYMBOLS:

I	1
V	5
X	10
L	50
C	100
D	500
M	1000

1	I	26	XXVI
2	II	27	XXVII
3	III	28	XXVIII
4	IV	29	XXIX
5	V	30	XXX
6	VI	31	XXXI
7	VII	32	XXXII
8	VIII	33	XXXIII
9	IX	34	XXXIV
10	X	35	XXXV
11	XI	36	XXXVI
12	XII	37	XXXVII
13	XIII	38	XXXVIII
14	XIV	39	XXXIX
15	XV	40	XL
16	XVI	41	XLI
17	XVII	42	XLII
18	XVIII	43	XLIII
19	XIX	44	XLIV
20	XX	45	XLV
21	XXI	46	XLVI
22	XXII	47	XLVII
23	XXIII	48	XLVIII
24	XXIV	49	XLIX
25	XXV	50	L

Why Did Paul Write This Letter to the Romans?

I

II

DESIRE

It was Paul's long-time goal to bring the gospel to Rome.

ROMANS 1:9-12

CARE

Paul heard tensions existed between Jewish and Gentile believers in Rome. They lacked a doctrinal foundation to sort out their differences. Paul wanted to address these issues that divided them.

ROMANS 9:30-10:4

PLAN

Paul intended to visit Rome as soon as he delivered an offering to the poor believers in Jerusalem.

ROMANS 15:25-29

VISION

Paul hoped Rome would become his base of operations if he was given the opportunity to take the gospel to Spain, as Antioch had been for his first three missionary journeys.

ROMANS 15:22-24

OPPORTUNITY

Paul knew his friend Phoebe could deliver his letter. During Paul's third missionary journey, Phoebe told Paul she was planning to visit his friends Priscilla and Aquila in Rome.

ROMANS 16:1-4

III IV V

The Roman Empire in Jesus' Day

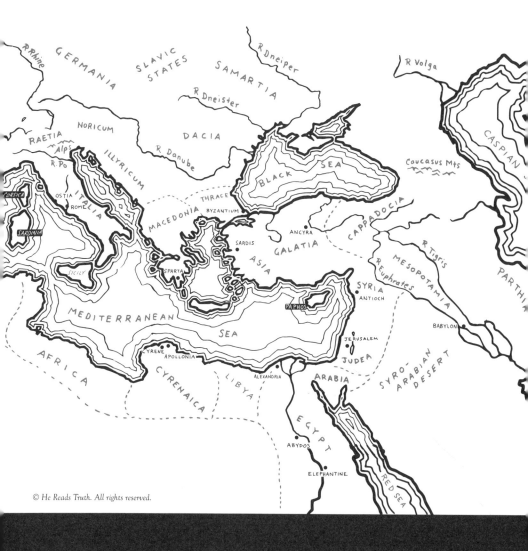

Romans 8:26-39
Psalm 44:17-22
Philippians 1:6
2 Thessalonians 2:14

The Believer's Triumph

DATE

²⁶ In the same way the Spirit also helps us in our weakness, because we do not know what to pray for as we should, but the Spirit himself intercedes for us with unspoken groanings. ²⁷ And he who searches our hearts knows the mind of the Spirit, because he intercedes for the saints according to the will of God.

²⁸ We know that all things work together for the good of those who love God, who are called according to his purpose. ²⁹ For those he foreknew he also predestined to be conformed to the image of his Son, so that he would be the firstborn among many brothers and sisters. ³⁰ And those he predestined, he also called; and those he called, he also justified; and those he justified, he also glorified.

The Believer's Triumph

³¹ What then are we to say about these things? If God is for us, who is against us? ³² He did not even spare his own Son but offered him up for us all. How will he not also with him grant us everything? ³³ Who can bring an accusation against God's elect? God is the one who justifies. ³⁴ Who is the one who condemns? Christ Jesus is the one who died, but even more, has been raised; he also is at the right hand of God and intercedes for us. ³⁵ Who can separate us from the love of Christ? Can affliction or distress or persecution or famine or nakedness or danger or sword? ³⁶ As it is written:

> Because of you
> we are being put to death all day long;
> we are counted as sheep to be slaughtered.

³⁷ No, in all these things we are more than conquerors through him who loved us. ³⁸ For I am persuaded that neither death nor life, nor angels nor rulers, nor things present nor things to come, nor powers, ³⁹ nor height nor depth, nor any other created thing will be able to separate us from the love of God that is in Christ Jesus our Lord.

PSALM 44:17-22

[17] All this has happened to us,

but we have not forgotten you

or betrayed your covenant.

[18] Our hearts have not turned back;

our steps have not strayed from your path.

[19] But you have crushed us in a haunt of jackals

and have covered us with deepest darkness.

[20] If we had forgotten the name of our God

and spread out our hands to a foreign god,

[21] wouldn't God have found this out,

since he knows the secrets of the heart?

[22] Because of you we are being put to death all day long;

we are counted as sheep to be slaughtered.

PHILIPPIANS 1:6

I am sure of this, that he who started a good work in you will carry it on to completion until the day of Christ Jesus.

2 THESSALONIANS 2:14

He called you to this through our gospel, so that you might obtain the glory of our Lord Jesus Christ.

RESPONSE

Romans 9:1-19
Exodus 32:30-32
Ephesians 1:3-6

God's Mercy and Compassion

Israel's Rejection Of Christ

¹ I speak the truth in Christ—I am not lying; my conscience testifies to me through the Holy Spirit— ² that I have great sorrow and unceasing anguish in my heart. ³ For I could wish that I myself were cursed and cut off from Christ for the benefit of my brothers and sisters, my own flesh and blood. ⁴ They are Israelites, and to them belong the adoption, the glory, the covenants, the giving of the law, the temple service, and the promises. ⁵ The ancestors are theirs, and from them, by physical descent, came the Christ, who is God over all, praised forever. Amen.

God's Gracious Election Of Israel

⁶ Now it is not as though the word of God has failed, because not all who are descended from Israel are Israel. ⁷ Neither are all of Abraham's children his descendants. On the contrary, your offspring will be traced through Isaac. ⁸ That is, it is not the children by physical descent who are God's children, but the children of the promise are considered to be the offspring. ⁹ For this is the statement of the promise: At this time I will come, and Sarah will have a son. ¹⁰ And not only that, but Rebekah conceived children through one man, our father Isaac. ¹¹ For though her sons had not been born yet or done anything good or bad, so that God's purpose according to election might stand— ¹² not from works but from the one who calls—she was told, The older will serve the younger. ¹³ As it is written: I have loved Jacob, but I have hated Esau.

God's Selection Is Just

¹⁴ What should we say then? Is there injustice with God? Absolutely not! ¹⁵ For he tells Moses, I will show mercy to whom I will show mercy, and I will have compassion on whom I will have compassion. ¹⁶ So then, it does not depend on human will or effort but on God who shows mercy. ¹⁷ For the Scripture tells Pharaoh, I raised you up for this reason so that I may display my power in you and that my name may be proclaimed in the whole earth. ¹⁸ So then, he has mercy on whom he wants to have mercy and he hardens whom he wants to harden.

[19] You will say to me, therefore, "Why then does he still find fault? For who can resist his will?"

EXODUS 32:30-32

[30] The following day Moses said to the people, "You have committed a grave sin. Now I will go up to the LORD; perhaps I will be able to atone for your sin."

[31] So Moses returned to the LORD and said, "Oh, these people have committed a grave sin; they have made a god of gold for themselves. [32] Now if you would only forgive their sin. But if not, please erase me from the book you have written."

EPHESIANS 1:3-6

[3] Blessed is the God and Father of our Lord Jesus Christ, who has blessed us with every spiritual blessing in the heavens in Christ. [4] For he chose us in him, before the foundation of the world, to be holy and blameless in love before him. [5] He predestined us to be adopted as sons through Jesus Christ for himself, according to the good pleasure of his will, [6] to the praise of his glorious grace that he lavished on us in the Beloved One.

RESPONSE

Romans 9:20-33
Jeremiah 18:1-6
Ephesians 1:11-14

Righteousness through Faith

DATE _____

²⁰ But who are you, a mere man, to talk back to God? Will what is formed say to the one who formed it, "Why did you make me like this?" ²¹ Or has the potter no right over the clay, to make from the same lump one piece of pottery for honor and another for dishonor? ²² And what if God, wanting to display his wrath and to make his power known, endured with much patience objects of wrath prepared for destruction? ²³ And what if he did this to make known the riches of his glory on objects of mercy that he prepared beforehand for glory— ²⁴ on us, the ones he also called, not only from the Jews but also from the Gentiles? ²⁵ As it also says in Hosea,

> I will call Not my People, my People,
> and she who is Unloved, Beloved.
> ²⁶ And it will be in the place where they were told,
> you are not my people,
> there they will be called sons of the living God.

²⁷ But Isaiah cries out concerning Israel,

> Though the number of Israelites
> is like the sand of the sea,
> only the remnant will be saved;
> ²⁸ since the Lord will execute his sentence
> completely and decisively on the earth.

²⁹ And just as Isaiah predicted:

> If the Lord of Hosts had not left us offspring,
> we would have become like Sodom,
> and we would have been made like Gomorrah.

Israel's Present State

³⁰ What should we say then? Gentiles, who did not pursue righteousness, have obtained righteousness—namely the righteousness that comes from faith. ³¹ But Israel, pursuing the law of righteousness, has not achieved the righteousness of the law. ³² Why is that? Because they did not pursue it by faith, but as if it were by works. They stumbled over the stumbling stone. ³³ As it is written,

> Look, I am putting a stone in Zion to stumble over
> and a rock to trip over,
> and the one who believes on him
> will not be put to shame.

JEREMIAH 18:1-6

Parable Of The Potter

¹ This is the word that came to Jeremiah from the LORD: ² "Go down at once to the potter's house; there I will reveal my words to you." ³ So I went down to the potter's house, and there he was, working away at the wheel. ⁴ But the jar that he was making from the clay became flawed in the potter's hand, so he made it into another jar, as it seemed right for him to do.

⁵ The word of the LORD came to me: ⁶ "House of Israel, can I not treat you as this potter treats his clay?"—this is the LORD's declaration. "Just like clay in the potter's hand, so are you in my hand, house of Israel."

EPHESIANS 1:11-14

¹¹ In him we have also received an inheritance, because we were predestined according to the plan of the one who works out everything in agreement with the purpose of his will, ¹² so that we who had already put our hope in Christ might bring praise to his glory.

[13] In him you also—when you heard the word of truth, the gospel of your salvation, and when you believed—were sealed in him with the promised Holy Spirit. [14] He is the down payment of our inheritance, until the redemption of the possession, to the praise of his glory.

RESPONSE

Romans 10
Isaiah 52:7
Joel 2:32
Galatians 3:7-14

The Message of Christ

DATE _____

Righteousness By Faith Alone

[1] Brothers and sisters, my heart's desire and prayer to God concerning them is for their salvation. [2] I can testify about them that they have zeal for God, but not according to knowledge. [3] Since they are ignorant of the righteousness of God and attempted to establish their own righteousness, they have not submitted to God's righteousness. [4] For Christ is the end of the law for righteousness to everyone who believes, [5] since Moses writes about the righteousness that is from the law: The one who does these things will live by them. [6] But the righteousness that comes from faith speaks like this: Do not say in your heart, "Who will go up to heaven?" that is, to bring Christ down [7] or, "Who will go down into the abyss?" that is, to bring Christ up from the dead. [8] On the contrary, what does it say? The message is near you, in your mouth and in your heart. This is the message of faith that we proclaim: [9] If you confess with your mouth, "Jesus is Lord," and believe in your heart that God raised him from the dead, you will be saved. [10] One believes with the heart, resulting in righteousness, and one confesses with the mouth, resulting in salvation. [11] For the Scripture says, Everyone who believes on him will not be put to shame, [12] since there is no distinction between Jew and Greek, because the same Lord of all richly blesses all who call on him. [13] For everyone who calls on the name of the Lord will be saved.

Israel's Rejection Of The Message

[14] How, then, can they call on him they have not believed in? And how can they believe without hearing about him? And how can they hear without a preacher? [15] And how can they preach unless they are sent? As it is written: How beautiful are the feet of those who bring good news. [16] But not all obeyed the gospel. For Isaiah says, Lord, who has believed our message? [17] So faith comes from what is heard, and what is heard comes through the message about Christ. [18] But I ask, "Did they not hear?" Yes, they did:

Their voice has gone out to the whole earth,
and their words to the ends of the world.

[19] But I ask, "Did Israel not understand?" First, Moses said,

> I will make you jealous
> of those who are not a nation;
> I will make you angry by a nation
> that lacks understanding.

[20] And Isaiah says boldly,

> I was found
> by those who were not looking for me;
> I revealed myself
> to those who were not asking for me.

[21] But to Israel he says, All day long I have held out my hands to a disobedient and defiant people.

ISAIAH 52:7

> How beautiful on the mountains
> are the feet of the herald,
> who proclaims peace,
> who brings news of good things,
> who proclaims salvation,
> who says to Zion, "Your God reigns!"

Then everyone who calls
on the name of the LORD will be saved,
for there will be an escape
for those on Mount Zion and in Jerusalem,
as the LORD promised,
among the survivors the LORD calls.

[7] You know, then, that those who have faith, these are Abraham's sons. [8] Now the Scripture saw in advance that God would justify the Gentiles by faith and proclaimed the gospel ahead of time to Abraham, saying, All the nations will be blessed through you. [9] Consequently those who have faith are blessed with Abraham, who had faith.

Law And Promise

[10] For all who rely on the works of the law are under a curse, because it is written, Everyone who does not do everything written in the book of the law is cursed. [11] Now it is clear that no one is justified before God by the law, because the righteous will live by faith. [12] But the law is not based on faith; instead, the one who does these things will live by them. [13] Christ redeemed us from the curse of the law by becoming a curse for us, because it is written, Cursed is everyone who is hung on a tree. [14] The purpose was that the blessing of Abraham would come to the Gentiles by Christ Jesus, so that we could receive the promised Spirit through faith.

RESPONSE

RESPONSE

Romans 11:1-24
Hosea 14:4-7
Ephesians 2:8-9

God's Kindness and Severity

DATE _____

Israel's Rejection Not Total

[1] I ask, then, has God rejected his people? Absolutely not! For I too am an Israelite, a descendant of Abraham, from the tribe of Benjamin. [2] God has not rejected his people whom he foreknew. Or don't you know what the Scripture says in the passage about Elijah—how he pleads with God against Israel? [3] Lord, they have killed your prophets and torn down your altars. I am the only one left, and they are trying to take my life! [4] But what was God's answer to him? I have left seven thousand for myself who have not bowed down to Baal. [5] In the same way, then, there is also at the present time a remnant chosen by grace. [6] Now if by grace, then it is not by works; otherwise grace ceases to be grace.

[7] What then? Israel did not find what it was looking for, but the elect did find it. The rest were hardened, [8] as it is written,

> God gave them a spirit of stupor,
> eyes that cannot see
> and ears that cannot hear,
> to this day.

[9] And David says,

> Let their table become a snare and a trap,
> a pitfall and a retribution to them.
> [10] Let their eyes be darkened so that they cannot see,
> and their backs be bent continually.

Israel's Rejection Not Final

[11] I ask, then, have they stumbled so as to fall? Absolutely not! On the contrary, by their transgression, salvation has come to the Gentiles to make Israel jealous. [12] Now if their transgression brings riches for the world, and their failure riches for the Gentiles, how much more will their fullness bring!

[13] Now I am speaking to you Gentiles. Insofar as I am an apostle to the Gentiles, I magnify my ministry, [14] if I might somehow make my own people jealous and save some of them. [15] For if their rejection brings reconciliation to the world, what will their acceptance mean but life from the dead? [16] Now if the firstfruits are holy, so is the whole batch. And if the root is holy, so are the branches.

[17] Now if some of the branches were broken off, and you, though a wild olive branch, were grafted in among them and have come to share in the rich root of the cultivated olive tree, [18] do not boast that you are better than those branches. But if you do boast—you do not sustain the root, but the root sustains you. [19] Then you will say, "Branches were broken off so that I might be grafted in." [20] True enough; they were broken off because of unbelief, but you stand by faith. Do not be arrogant, but beware, [21] because if God did not spare the natural branches, he will not spare you either. [22] Therefore, consider God's kindness and severity: severity toward those who have fallen but God's kindness toward you—if you remain in his kindness. Otherwise you too will be cut off. [23] And even they, if they do not remain in unbelief, will be grafted in, because God has the power to graft them in again. [24] For if you were cut off from your native wild olive tree and against nature were grafted into a cultivated olive tree, how much more will these—the natural branches—be grafted into their own olive tree?

HOSEA 14:4-7

A Promise Of Restoration

[4] I will heal their apostasy;
I will freely love them,
for my anger will have turned from him.
[5] I will be like the dew to Israel;
he will blossom like the lily
and take root like the cedars of Lebanon.

⁶ His new branches will spread,

and his splendor will be like the olive tree,

his fragrance, like the forest of Lebanon.

⁷ The people will return and live beneath his shade.

They will grow grain

and blossom like the vine.

His renown will be like the wine of Lebanon.

EPHESIANS 2:8-9

⁸ For you are saved by grace through faith, and this is not from yourselves; it is God's gift — ⁹ not from works, so that no one can boast.

RESPONSE

RESPONSE

Grace Day

Take this day as an opportunity to catch up on your reading, pray, and rest in the presence of the Lord. If you'd like, play or sing this hymn inspired by the book of Romans.

Ephesians 2:8-9

For you are saved by grace through faith, and this is not from yourselves; it is God's gift — not from works, so that no one can boast.

DATE

JESUS, LOVER OF MY SOUL

ROMANS 8:35-39

Text: Charles Wesley, 1738 | Tune: Joseph Parry, 1876

Discussion Questions

The book of Romans is a thorough and succinct presentation of the message of Jesus Christ—the essential gospel. In chapter 8, Paul asks a series of open-ended questions which help us consider the effect of this gospel in the life of a believer. Each week we will return to this passage and this string of questions to explore what each one means and how to apply them.

Read Romans 8:18-39 and discuss the following questions as a group, or use them as journaling prompts to work and pray through on your own.

WHO CAN BRING AN ACCUSATION AGAINST GOD'S ELECT? GOD IS THE ONE WHO JUSTIFIES. WHO IS THE ONE WHO CONDEMNS? CHRIST JESUS IS THE ONE WHO DIED, BUT EVEN MORE, HAS BEEN RAISED; HE ALSO IS AT THE RIGHT HAND OF GOD AND INTERCEDES FOR US.

ROMANS 8:33-34

I   What does it mean that Christ intercedes for us? Who does He intercede to? What does He intercede about?

II   What are some of the voices of accusation and condemnation you struggle with most? Why?

III   What is the hope promised in these verses?

Weekly Truth

Memorizing Scripture is one of the best ways to carry God-breathed truth, instruction, and reproof wherever we go.

As we read through Romans together, we are memorizing the steps in the Romans Road to salvation. The fourth step shows our **response** *to the solution God provides: confess and believe.*

Romans 10:9-10

If you confess with your mouth, "Jesus is Lord," and believe in your heart that God raised him from the dead, you will be saved. One believes with the heart, resulting in righteousness, and one confesses with the mouth, resulting in salvation.

DATE

NOTES

Romans 11:25-36
Isaiah 40:13-15
1 Corinthians 12:4-11

The Depth of God's Wisdom

DATE

²⁵ I don't want you to be ignorant of this mystery, brothers and sisters, so that you will not be conceited: A partial hardening has come upon Israel until the fullness of the Gentiles has come in. ²⁶ And in this way all Israel will be saved, as it is written,

The Deliverer will come from Zion;

he will turn godlessness away from Jacob.

²⁷ And this will be my covenant with them

when I take away their sins.

²⁸ Regarding the gospel, they are enemies for your advantage, but regarding election, they are loved because of the patriarchs, ²⁹ since God's gracious gifts and calling are irrevocable. ³⁰ As you once disobeyed God but now have received mercy through their disobedience, ³¹ so they too have now disobeyed, resulting in mercy to you, so that they also may now receive mercy. ³² For God has imprisoned all in disobedience so that he may have mercy on all.

A Hymn Of Praise

³³ Oh, the depth of the riches

both of the wisdom and of the knowledge of God!

How unsearchable his judgments

and untraceable his ways!

³⁴ For who has known the mind of the Lord?

Or who has been his counselor?

³⁵ And who has ever given to God,

that he should be repaid?

³⁶ For from him and through him

and to him are all things.

To him be the glory forever. Amen.

¹³ Who has directed the Spirit of the LORD,
or who gave him counsel?
¹⁴ Who did he consult?
Who gave him understanding
and taught him the paths of justice?
Who taught him knowledge
and showed him the way of understanding?
¹⁵ Look, the nations are like a drop in a bucket;
they are considered as a speck of dust on the scales;
he lifts up the islands like fine dust.

1 CORINTHIANS 12:4-11

⁴ Now there are different gifts, but the same Spirit. ⁵ There are different ministries, but the same Lord. ⁶ And there are different activities, but the same God produces each gift in each person. ⁷ A manifestation of the Spirit is given to each person for the common good: ⁸ to one is given a message of wisdom through the Spirit, to another, a message of knowledge by the same Spirit, ⁹ to another, faith by the same Spirit, to another, gifts of healing by the one Spirit, ¹⁰ to another, the performing of miracles, to another, prophecy, to another, distinguishing between spirits, to another, different kinds of tongues, to another, interpretation of tongues. ¹¹ One and the same Spirit is active in all these, distributing to each person as he wills.

RESPONSE

Romans 12:1-8
Hebrews 13:15-16
Ephesians 4:1-16

A Living Sacrifice

[1] Therefore, brothers and sisters, in view of the mercies of God, I urge you to present your bodies as a living sacrifice, holy and pleasing to God; this is your true worship. [2] Do not be conformed to this age, but be transformed by the renewing of your mind, so that you may discern what is the good, pleasing, and perfect will of God.

Many Gifts But One Body

[3] For by the grace given to me, I tell everyone among you not to think of himself more highly than he should think. Instead, think sensibly, as God has distributed a measure of faith to each one. [4] Now as we have many parts in one body, and all the parts do not have the same function, [5] in the same way we who are many are one body in Christ and individually members of one another. [6] According to the grace given to us, we have different gifts: If prophecy, use it according to the proportion of one's faith; [7] if service, use it in service; if teaching, in teaching; [8] if exhorting, in exhortation; giving, with generosity; leading, with diligence; showing mercy, with cheerfulness.

[15] Therefore, through him let us continually offer up to God a sacrifice of praise, that is, the fruit of lips that confess his name. [16] Don't neglect to do what is good and to share, for God is pleased with such sacrifices.

Unity And Diversity In The Body Of Christ

[1] Therefore I, the prisoner in the Lord, urge you to live worthy of the calling you have received, [2] with all humility and gentleness, with patience, bearing with one another in love, [3] making every effort to keep the unity of the Spirit through the bond of peace. [4] There is one body and one Spirit—just as you were called to one hope at your calling— [5] one Lord, one faith, one baptism, [6] one God and Father of all, who is above all and through all and in all.

⁷ Now grace was given to each one of us according to the measure of Christ's gift. ⁸ For it says:

> When he ascended on high,
> he took the captives captive;
> he gave gifts to people.

⁹ But what does "he ascended" mean except that he also descended to the lower parts of the earth? ¹⁰ The one who descended is also the one who ascended far above all the heavens, to fill all things. ¹¹ And he himself gave some to be apostles, some prophets, some evangelists, some pastors and teachers, ¹² equipping the saints for the work of ministry, to build up the body of Christ, ¹³ until we all reach unity in the faith and in the knowledge of God's Son, growing into maturity with a stature measured by Christ's fullness. ¹⁴ Then we will no longer be little children, tossed by the waves and blown around by every wind of teaching, by human cunning with cleverness in the techniques of deceit. ¹⁵ But speaking the truth in love, let us grow in every way into him who is the head—Christ. ¹⁶ From him the whole body, fitted and knit together by every supporting ligament, promotes the growth of the body for building up itself in love by the proper working of each individual part.

RESPONSE

Romans 12:9-21
Matthew 5:44-47
1 Corinthians 4:6-13

Christian Ethics

DATE _____

Christian Ethics

⁹ Let love be without hypocrisy. Detest evil; cling to what is good. ¹⁰ Love one another deeply as brothers and sisters. Outdo one another in showing honor. ¹¹ Do not lack diligence in zeal; be fervent in the Spirit; serve the Lord. ¹² Rejoice in hope; be patient in affliction; be persistent in prayer. ¹³ Share with the saints in their needs; pursue hospitality. ¹⁴ Bless those who persecute you; bless and do not curse. ¹⁵ Rejoice with those who rejoice; weep with those who weep. ¹⁶ Live in harmony with one another. Do not be proud; instead, associate with the humble. Do not be wise in your own estimation. ¹⁷ Do not repay anyone evil for evil. Give careful thought to do what is honorable in everyone's eyes. ¹⁸ If possible, as far as it depends on you, live at peace with everyone. ¹⁹ Friends, do not avenge yourselves; instead, leave room for God's wrath, because it is written, Vengeance belongs to me; I will repay, says the Lord. ²⁰ But

> If your enemy is hungry, feed him.
> If he is thirsty, give him something to drink.
> For in so doing
> you will be heaping fiery coals on his head.

²¹ Do not be conquered by evil, but conquer evil with good.

⁴⁴ "But I tell you, love your enemies and pray for those who persecute you, ⁴⁵ so that you may be children of your Father in heaven. For he causes his sun to rise on the evil and the good, and sends rain on the righteous and the unrighteous. ⁴⁶ For if you love those who love you, what reward will you have? Don't even the tax collectors do the same? ⁴⁷ And if you greet only your brothers and sisters, what are you doing out of the ordinary? Don't even the Gentiles do the same?"

The Apostles' Example Of Humility

[6] Now, brothers and sisters, I have applied these things to myself and Apollos for your benefit, so that you may learn from us the meaning of the saying: "Nothing beyond what is written." The purpose is that none of you will be arrogant, favoring one person over another. [7] For who makes you so superior? What do you have that you didn't receive? If, in fact, you did receive it, why do you boast as if you hadn't received it? [8] You are already full! You are already rich! You have begun to reign as kings without us—and I wish you did reign, so that we could also reign with you! [9] For I think God has displayed us, the apostles, in last place, like men condemned to die: We have become a spectacle to the world, both to angels and to people. [10] We are fools for Christ, but you are wise in Christ! We are weak, but you are strong! You are distinguished, but we are dishonored! [11] Up to the present hour we are both hungry and thirsty; we are poorly clothed, roughly treated, homeless; [12] we labor, working with our own hands. When we are reviled, we bless; when we are persecuted, we endure it; [13] when we are slandered, we respond graciously. Even now, we are like the scum of the earth, like everyone's garbage.

RESPONSE

Romans 13
Daniel 2:19-23
Hebrews 11:32-40

Christian Duty

DATE

A Christian's Duties To The State

[1] Let everyone submit to the governing authorities, since there is no authority except from God, and the authorities that exist are instituted by God. [2] So then, the one who resists the authority is opposing God's command, and those who oppose it will bring judgment on themselves. [3] For rulers are not a terror to good conduct, but to bad. Do you want to be unafraid of the authority? Do what is good, and you will have its approval. [4] For it is God's servant for your good. But if you do wrong, be afraid, because it does not carry the sword for no reason. For it is God's servant, an avenger that brings wrath on the one who does wrong. [5] Therefore, you must submit, not only because of wrath but also because of your conscience. [6] And for this reason you pay taxes, since the authorities are God's servants, continually attending to these tasks. [7] Pay your obligations to everyone: taxes to those you owe taxes, tolls to those you owe tolls, respect to those you owe respect, and honor to those you owe honor.

Love, Our Primary Duty

[8] Do not owe anyone anything, except to love one another, for the one who loves another has fulfilled the law. [9] The commandments, Do not commit adultery; do not murder; do not steal; do not covet; and any other commandment, are summed up by this commandment: Love your neighbor as yourself. [10] Love does no wrong to a neighbor. Love, therefore, is the fulfillment of the law.

Put On Christ

[11] Besides this, since you know the time, it is already the hour for you to wake up from sleep, because now our salvation is nearer than when we first believed. [12] The night is nearly over, and the day is near; so let us discard the deeds of darkness and put on the armor of light. [13] Let us walk with decency, as in the daytime: not in carousing and drunkenness; not in sexual impurity and promiscuity; not in quarreling and jealousy. [14] But put on the Lord Jesus Christ, and don't make plans to gratify the desires of the flesh.

DANIEL 2:19-23

[19] The mystery was then revealed to Daniel in a vision at night, and Daniel praised the God of the heavens [20] and declared:

> May the name of God
> be praised forever and ever,
> for wisdom and power belong to him.
> [21] He changes the times and seasons;
> he removes kings and establishes kings.
> He gives wisdom to the wise
> and knowledge to those
> who have understanding.
> [22] He reveals the deep and hidden things;
> he knows what is in the darkness,
> and light dwells with him.
> [23] I offer thanks and praise to you,
> God of my fathers,
> because you have given me
> wisdom and power.
> And now you have let me know
> what we asked of you,
> for you have let us know
> the king's mystery.

HEBREWS 11:32-40

[32] And what more can I say? Time is too short for me to tell about Gideon, Barak, Samson, Jephthah, David, Samuel, and the prophets, [33] who by faith conquered kingdoms, administered justice, obtained promises, shut the mouths of lions, [34] quenched the raging of fire, escaped the edge of the sword, gained strength in weakness, became mighty in battle, and put foreign

armies to flight. ³⁵ Women received their dead, raised to life again. Other people were tortured, not accepting release, so that they might gain a better resurrection. ³⁶ Others experienced mockings and scourgings, as well as bonds and imprisonment. ³⁷ They were stoned, they were sawed in two, they died by the sword, they wandered about in sheepskins, in goatskins, destitute, afflicted, and mistreated. ³⁸ The world was not worthy of them. They wandered in deserts and on mountains, hiding in caves and holes in the ground.

³⁹ All these were approved through their faith, but they did not receive what was promised, ⁴⁰ since God had provided something better for us, so that they would not be made perfect without us.

RESPONSE

RESPONSE

Romans 14:1-12
Colossians 2:16-17
Hebrews 10:19-25

The Law
of Liberty

DATE _____

The Law Of Liberty

[1] Accept anyone who is weak in faith, but don't argue about disputed matters. [2] One person believes he may eat anything, while one who is weak eats only vegetables. [3] One who eats must not look down on one who does not eat, and one who does not eat must not judge one who does, because God has accepted him. [4] Who are you to judge another's household servant? Before his own Lord he stands or falls. And he will stand, because the Lord is able to make him stand.

[5] One person judges one day to be more important than another day. Someone else judges every day to be the same. Let each one be fully convinced in his own mind. [6] Whoever observes the day, observes it for the honor of the Lord. Whoever eats, eats for the Lord, since he gives thanks to God; and whoever does not eat, it is for the Lord that he does not eat it, and he gives thanks to God. [7] For none of us lives for himself, and no one dies for himself. [8] If we live, we live for the Lord; and if we die, we die for the Lord. Therefore, whether we live or die, we belong to the Lord. [9] Christ died and returned to life for this: that he might be Lord over both the dead and the living. [10] But you, why do you judge your brother or sister? Or you, why do you despise your brother or sister? For we will all stand before the judgment seat of God. [11] For it is written,

As I live, says the Lord,
every knee will bow to me,
and every tongue will give praise to God.

[12] So then, each of us will give an account of himself to God.

COLOSSIANS 2:16-17

[16] Therefore, don't let anyone judge you in regard to food and drink or in the matter of a festival or a new moon or a Sabbath day. [17] These are a shadow of what was to come; the substance is Christ.

Exhortations To Godliness

[19] Therefore, brothers and sisters, since we have boldness to enter the sanctuary through the blood of Jesus— [20] he has inaugurated for us a new and living way through the curtain (that is, through his flesh)— [21] and since we have a great high priest over the house of God, [22] let us draw near with a true heart in full assurance of faith, with our hearts sprinkled clean from an evil conscience and our bodies washed in pure water. [23] Let us hold on to the confession of our hope without wavering, since he who promised is faithful. [24] And let us watch out for one another to provoke love and good works, [25] not neglecting to gather together, as some are in the habit of doing, but encouraging each other, and all the more as you see the day approaching.

RESPONSE

Grace
Day

Take this day as an opportunity to catch up on your reading, pray, and rest in the presence of the Lord. If you'd like, play or sing this hymn inspired by the book of Romans.

Hebrews 13:16

Don't neglect to do what is good and to share, for God is pleased with such sacrifices.

DATE

JUST AS I AM

ROMANS 10:9

come to Thee, O Lamb of God, I come, I come.
cleanse each spot, O Lamb of God, I come, I come.
in, with - out, O Lamb of God, I come, I come.
I be - lieve, O Lamb of God, I come, I come.

Text: Charlotte Elliott, 1836 | Tune: William B. Bradbury, 1849

Discussion Questions

The book of Romans is a thorough and succinct presentation of the message of Jesus Christ–the essential gospel. In chapter 8, Paul asks a series of open-ended questions which help us consider the effect of this gospel in the life of a believer. Each week we will return to this passage and this string of questions to explore what each one means and how to apply them.

Read Romans 8:18-39 and discuss the following questions as a group, or use them as journaling prompts to work and pray through on your own.

WHO CAN SEPARATE US FROM THE LOVE OF CHRIST? CAN AFFLICTION OR DISTRESS OR PERSECUTION OR FAMINE OR NAKEDNESS OR DANGER OR SWORD?

ROMANS 8:35

I What does it mean to be separated from Christ? What does it mean to not be separated from Christ?

II What would you add to Paul's list of threats? What do you feel threatens to separate you from the love of Christ?

III Why can we rest assured that we will not be separated from the love of Christ?

Weekly Truth

Memorizing Scripture is a way to carry God's Word with you wherever you go, keeping God-breathed instruction, reproof, and truth in your heart and mind each day.

As we read through Romans together, we are memorizing the steps in the Romans Road to salvation. The fifth and final step declares the **assurance** *that we have in Christ Jesus.*

Romans 10:13 | For everyone who calls on the name of the Lord will be saved.

DATE

NOTES

Romans 14:13-23
1 Corinthians 8:8-13
Ephesians 4:25-32
Ephesians 5:1-2

The Law of Love

DATE _____

The Law Of Love

[13] Therefore, let us no longer judge one another. Instead decide never to put a stumbling block or pitfall in the way of your brother or sister. [14] I know and am persuaded in the Lord Jesus that nothing is unclean in itself. Still, to someone who considers a thing to be unclean, to that one it is unclean. [15] For if your brother or sister is hurt by what you eat, you are no longer walking according to love. Do not destroy, by what you eat, someone for whom Christ died. [16] Therefore, do not let your good be slandered, [17] for the kingdom of God is not eating and drinking, but righteousness, peace, and joy in the Holy Spirit. [18] Whoever serves Christ in this way is acceptable to God and receives human approval.

[19] So then, let us pursue what promotes peace and what builds up one another. [20] Do not tear down God's work because of food. Everything is clean, but it is wrong to make someone fall by what he eats. [21] It is a good thing not to eat meat, or drink wine, or do anything that makes your brother or sister stumble. [22] Whatever you believe about these things, keep between yourself and God. Blessed is the one who does not condemn himself by what he approves. [23] But whoever doubts stands condemned if he eats, because his eating is not from faith, and everything that is not from faith is sin.

[8] Food will not bring us close to God. We are not worse off if we don't eat, and we are not better if we do eat. [9] But be careful that this right of yours in no way becomes a stumbling block to the weak. [10] For if someone sees you, the one who has knowledge, dining in an idol's temple, won't his weak conscience be encouraged to eat food offered to idols? [11] So the weak person, the brother or

sister for whom Christ died, is ruined by your knowledge. [12] Now when you sin like this against brothers and sisters and wound their weak conscience, you are sinning against Christ. [13] Therefore, if food causes my brother or sister to fall, I will never again eat meat, so that I won't cause my brother or sister to fall.

EPHESIANS 4:25-32

[25] Therefore, putting away lying, speak the truth, each one to his neighbor, because we are members of one another. [26] Be angry and do not sin. Don't let the sun go down on your anger, [27] and don't give the devil an opportunity. [28] Let the thief no longer steal. Instead, he is to do honest work with his own hands, so that he has something to share with anyone in need. [29] No foul language should come from your mouth, but only what is good for building up someone in need, so that it gives grace to those who hear. [30] And don't grieve God's Holy Spirit. You were sealed by him for the day of redemption. [31] Let all bitterness, anger and wrath, shouting and slander be removed from you, along with all malice. [32] And be kind and compassionate to one another, forgiving one another, just as God also forgave you in Christ.

EPHESIANS 5:1-2

[1] Therefore, be imitators of God, as dearly loved children, [2] and walk in love, as Christ also loved us and gave himself for us, a sacrificial and fragrant offering to God.

RESPONSE

DAY 37

Romans 15:1-21
2 Samuel 22:50-51
Psalm 117

Glorifying God Together

DATE

Pleasing Others, Not Ourselves

[1] Now we who are strong have an obligation to bear the weaknesses of those without strength, and not to please ourselves. [2] Each one of us is to please his neighbor for his good, to build him up. [3] For even Christ did not please himself. On the contrary, as it is written, The insults of those who insult you have fallen on me. [4] For whatever was written in the past was written for our instruction, so that we may have hope through endurance and through the encouragement from the Scriptures. [5] Now may the God who gives endurance and encouragement grant you to live in harmony with one another, according to Christ Jesus, [6] so that you may glorify the God and Father of our Lord Jesus Christ with one mind and one voice.

Glorifying God Together

[7] Therefore accept one another, just as Christ also accepted you, to the glory of God. [8] For I say that Christ became a servant of the circumcised on behalf of God's truth, to confirm the promises to the fathers, [9] and so that Gentiles may glorify God for his mercy. As it is written,

Therefore I will praise you among the Gentiles,
and I will sing praise to your name.

[10] Again it says, Rejoice, you Gentiles, with his people! [11] And again,

Praise the Lord, all you Gentiles;
let all the peoples praise him!

[12] And again, Isaiah says,

The root of Jesse will appear,
the one who rises to rule the Gentiles;
the Gentiles will hope in him.

[13] Now may the God of hope fill you with all joy and peace as you believe so that you may overflow with hope by the power of the Holy Spirit.

From Jerusalem To Illyricum

[14] My brothers and sisters, I myself am convinced about you that you also are full of goodness, filled with all knowledge, and able to instruct one another. [15] Nevertheless, I have written to remind you more boldly on some points because of the grace given me by God [16] to be a minister of Christ Jesus to the Gentiles, serving as a priest of the gospel of God. My purpose is that the Gentiles may be an acceptable offering, sanctified by the Holy Spirit. [17] Therefore I have reason to boast in Christ Jesus regarding what pertains to God. [18] For I would not dare say anything except what Christ has accomplished through me by word and deed for the obedience of the Gentiles, [19] by the power of miraculous signs and wonders, and by the power of God's Spirit. As a result, I have fully proclaimed the gospel of Christ from Jerusalem all the way around to Illyricum. [20] My aim is to preach the gospel where Christ has not been named, so that I will not build on someone else's foundation, [21] but, as it is written,

Those who were not told about him will see,
and those who have not heard will understand.

2 SAMUEL 22:50-51

[50] Therefore I will give thanks to you among the nations, LORD;
I will sing praises about your name.
[51] He is a tower of salvation for his king;
he shows loyalty to his anointed,
to David and his descendants forever.

PSALM 117

Universal Call To Praise

1 Praise the LORD, all nations!
Glorify him, all peoples!
2 For his faithful love to us is great;
the LORD's faithfulness endures forever.
Hallelujah!

RESPONSE

Romans 15:22-33
Isaiah 52:14-15
Hebrews 2:2-4

The Blessing of Christ

DATE

Paul's Travel Plans

²² That is why I have been prevented many times from coming to you. ²³ But now I no longer have any work to do in these regions, and I have strongly desired for many years to come to you ²⁴ whenever I travel to Spain. For I hope to see you when I pass through and to be assisted by you for my journey there, once I have first enjoyed your company for a while. ²⁵ Right now I am traveling to Jerusalem to serve the saints, ²⁶ because Macedonia and Achaia were pleased to make a contribution for the poor among the saints in Jerusalem. ²⁷ Yes, they were pleased, and indeed are indebted to them. For if the Gentiles have shared in their spiritual benefits, then they are obligated to minister to them in material needs. ²⁸ So when I have finished this and safely delivered the funds to them, I will visit you on the way to Spain. ²⁹ I know that when I come to you, I will come in the fullness of the blessing of Christ.

³⁰ Now I appeal to you, brothers and sisters, through our Lord Jesus Christ and through the love of the Spirit, to strive together with me in fervent prayers to God on my behalf. ³¹ Pray that I may be rescued from the unbelievers in Judea, that my ministry to Jerusalem may be acceptable to the saints, ³² and that, by God's will, I may come to you with joy and be refreshed together with you.

³³ May the God of peace be with all of you. Amen.

¹⁴ Just as many were appalled at you —
his appearance was so disfigured
that he did not look like a man,
and his form did not resemble a human being —
¹⁵ so he will sprinkle many nations.
Kings will shut their mouths because of him,
for they will see what had not been told them,
and they will understand what they had not heard.

[2] For if the message spoken through angels was legally binding and every transgression and disobedience received a just punishment, [3] how will we escape if we neglect such a great salvation? This salvation had its beginning when it was spoken of by the Lord, and it was confirmed to us by those who heard him. [4] At the same time, God also testified by signs and wonders, various miracles, and distributions of gifts from the Holy Spirit according to his will.

RESPONSE

DAY 39

Romans 16:1-16
John 13:16
1 Peter 5:14

Greet One Another

DATE _____

Paul's Commendation Of Phoebe

[1] I commend to you our sister Phoebe, who is a servant of the church in Cenchreae. [2] So you should welcome her in the Lord in a manner worthy of the saints and assist her in whatever matter she may require your help. For indeed she has been a benefactor of many—and of me also.

Greeting To Roman Christians

[3] Give my greetings to Prisca and Aquila, my coworkers in Christ Jesus, [4] who risked their own necks for my life. Not only do I thank them, but so do all the Gentile churches. [5] Greet also the church that meets in their home. Greet my dear friend Epaenetus, who is the first convert to Christ from Asia. [6] Greet Mary, who has worked very hard for you. [7] Greet Andronicus and Junia, my fellow Jews and fellow prisoners. They are noteworthy in the eyes of the apostles, and they were also in Christ before me. [8] Greet Ampliatus, my dear friend in the Lord. [9] Greet Urbanus, our coworker in Christ, and my dear friend Stachys. [10] Greet Apelles, who is approved in Christ. Greet those who belong to the household of Aristobulus. [11] Greet Herodion, my fellow Jew. Greet those who belong to the household of Narcissus who are in the Lord. [12] Greet Tryphaena and Tryphosa, who have worked hard in the Lord. Greet my dear friend Persis, who has worked very hard in the Lord. [13] Greet Rufus, chosen in the Lord; also his mother—and mine. [14] Greet Asyncritus, Phlegon, Hermes, Patrobas, Hermas, and the brothers and sisters who are with them. [15] Greet Philologus and Julia, Nereus and his sister, and Olympas, and all the saints who are with them. [16] Greet one another with a holy kiss. All the churches of Christ send you greetings.

"Truly I tell you, a servant is not greater than his master, and a messenger is not greater than the one who sent him."

1 PETER 5:14

Greet one another with a kiss of love. Peace to all of you who are in Christ.

RESPONSE

DAY 40

Romans 16:17-27
Matthew 7:15-20
Jude 24-25

Glory to God

Warning Against Divisive People

[17] Now I urge you, brothers and sisters, to watch out for those who create divisions and obstacles contrary to the teaching that you learned. Avoid them, [18] because such people do not serve our Lord Christ but their own appetites. They deceive the hearts of the unsuspecting with smooth talk and flattering words.

Paul's Gracious Conclusion

[19] The report of your obedience has reached everyone. Therefore I rejoice over you, but I want you to be wise about what is good, and yet innocent about what is evil. [20] The God of peace will soon crush Satan under your feet. The grace of our Lord Jesus be with you.

[21] Timothy, my coworker, and Lucius, Jason, and Sosipater, my fellow countrymen, greet you.

[22] I Tertius, who wrote this letter, greet you in the Lord.

[23] Gaius, who is host to me and to the whole church, greets you. Erastus, the city treas-urer, and our brother Quartus greet you.

Glory To God

[25] Now to him who is able to strengthen you according to my gospel and the proclamation about Jesus Christ, according to the revelation of the mystery kept silent for long ages [26] but now revealed and made known through the prophetic Scriptures, according to the command of the eternal God to advance the obedience of faith among all the Gentiles— [27] to the only wise God, through Jesus Christ—to him be the glory forever! Amen.

[15] "Be on your guard against false prophets who come to you in sheep's clothing but inwardly are ravaging wolves. [16] You'll recognize them by their fruit. Are grapes gathered from thornbushes or figs from thistles? [17] In the same way, every good tree produces good fruit, but a bad tree produces bad fruit. [18] A good tree can't produce bad fruit; neither can a bad tree produce good fruit. [19] Every tree that doesn't produce good fruit is cut down and thrown into the fire. [20] So you'll recognize them by their fruit."

[24] Now to him who is able to protect you from stumbling and to make you stand in the presence of his glory, without blemish and with great joy, [25] to the only God our Savior, through Jesus Christ our Lord, be glory, majesty, power, and authority before all time, now and forever. Amen.

RESPONSE

DAY 41

Grace Day

Take this day as an opportunity to catch up on your reading, pray, and rest in the presence of the Lord. If you'd like, play or sing this hymn inspired by the book of Romans.

Ephesians 5:1-2

Therefore, be imitators of God, as dearly loved children, and walk in love, as Christ also loved us and gave himself for us, a sacrificial and fragrant offering to God.

DATE

TAKE MY LIFE AND LET IT BE

ROMANS 12:1

1 Take my life and let it be con-se-crat-ed,
2 Take my hands and let them move at the im-pulse
3 Take my voice and let me sing al-ways, on-ly,
4 Take my sil-ver and my gold; not a mite would

Lord, to Thee. Take my mo-ments and my days; let them
of Thy love. Take my feet and let them be swift and
for my King. Take my lips and let them be filled with
I with-hold. Take my in-tel-lect and use ev-ery

flow in end-less praise, let them flow in end-less praise.
beau-ti-ful for Thee, swift and beau-ti-ful for Thee.
mes-sag-es from Thee, filled with mes-sag-es from Thee.
power as Thou shalt choose, ev-ery power as thou shalt choose.

5 Take my will and make it Thine;
it shall be no longer mine.
Take my heart—it is Thine own;
it shall be Thy royal throne,
it shall be Thy royal throne.

6 Take my love; my Lord, I pour
at Thy feet its treasure store.
Take myself, and I will be
ever, only, all for Thee,
ever, only, all for Thee.

Text: Frances R. Havergal, 1874 | Tune: H. A. Cesar Malan, 1827

Discussion Questions

The book of Romans is a thorough and succinct presentation of the message of Jesus Christ–the essential gospel. In chapter 8, Paul asks a series of open-ended questions which help us consider the effect of this gospel in the life of a believer. Each week we will return to this passage and this string of questions to explore what each one means and how to apply them.

Read Romans 8:18-39 and discuss the following questions as a group, or use them as journaling prompts to work and pray through on your own.

NO, IN ALL THESE THINGS WE ARE MORE THAN CONQUERORS THROUGH HIM WHO LOVED US. FOR I AM PERSUADED THAT NEITHER DEATH NOR LIFE, NOR ANGELS NOR RULERS, NOR THINGS PRESENT NOR THINGS TO COME, NOR POWERS, NOR HEIGHT NOR DEPTH, NOR ANY OTHER CREATED THING WILL BE ABLE TO SEPARATE US FROM THE LOVE OF GOD THAT IS IN CHRIST JESUS OUR LORD.

ROMANS 8:37-39

I   How would you express these verses in your own words? What is being said here?

II   These verses speak of the reality of a spiritual realm—angels and powers. How much do you think about spiritual forces, and what role do you think they play in your life?

III   In these verses, Paul says he is "persuaded" (other translations say "certain") that nothing can separate Christians from the love of Christ. What role does certainty play in the Christian life? When it comes to faith in Christ, of what can we be certain? Name at least three things.

Weekly Truth

Memorizing Scripture is a way to carry God's Word with you wherever you go, keeping God-breathed instruction, reproof, and truth in your heart and mind each day.

Now that we've memorized the Romans Road for salvation, let's commit to memory this **benediction** celebrating the completed work of Christ.

Romans 15:13

Now may the God of hope fill you with all joy and peace as you believe so that you may overflow with hope by the power of the Holy Spirit.

DATE

NOTES

Now may the God of hope fill you with all joy and peace as you believe so that you may overflow with hope by the power of the Holy Spirit.

ROMANS 15:13

FOR THE RECORD

ROMANS

Where did I study?

- ☐ HOME
- ☐ OFFICE
- ☐ CHURCH
- ☐ SCHOOL
- ☐ COFFEE SHOP
- ☐ OTHER:

_____

WHAT WAS I LISTENING TO?

Song: _____

Artist: _____

Album: _____

When did I have my best studying success?

- ☐ MORNING
- ☐ AFTERNOON
- ☐ NIGHT
- ☐ OTHER:

_____

What did I hope to get out of this study?

_____

_____

_____

_____

What was happening in the world?

_____

_____

_____

_____

_____

_____

WHAT WAS MY BIGGEST TAKEAWAY?

IN THIS STUDY, I LEARNED:

1

2

3

END DATE _____ / _____ / _____

COLOPHON

This book was printed offset in Nashville, Tennessee, on 70# Husky under the direction of He Reads Truth. Fonts used include Goudy Old Style, Knockout, Gotham, and Garamond. Cover is 100# Cougar Opaque with a soft touch lamination and 3/8" radius rounded corners.

EDITORS-IN-CHIEF

Raechel Myers and Amanda Bible Williams

MANAGING EDITOR

Rebecca Faires

EDITORS

Russ Ramsey and Kara Gause

CREATIVE DIRECTOR

Ryan Myers

DESIGN

Kelsea Allen

PRODUCTION DESIGN

Julie Allen

COLOR PHOTOGRAPHY

Brant Bauman

MAP ILLUSTRATIONS

Caleb Faires

THEOLOGICAL OVERSIGHT

Russ Ramsey, MDiv., ThM. and Nate Shurden, MDiv.

SUBSCRIPTION INQUIRIES

orders@hereadstruth.com